GROW RICH THINKING
Mindset + Action = Outrageous Achievement

LESLIE ZANN
FOREWORD BY DAVID MELTZER

Copyright © 2019 by Leslie Zann.

All rights reserved. Printed in the United States of America. No part of this publication may be reproduced, stored in a retrieval system, or transmitted in any form or by any means, electronic, mechanical, photocopying, recording or otherwise without the written permission of the author.

Disclaimer: This book is designed to provide information about the subject matter covered. It is sold with the understanding that the publisher and author are not engaged in rendering legal, accounting or other professional services. If legal or other expert assistance is required, the services of a competent professional should be sought. It is not the purpose of this book to provide or reprint all the information that is otherwise available to the author and/or publisher, but to complement, amplify, supplement and direct you to other information and texts readily available. You are urged to read all the available material, learn as much as possible about the subject and to tailor the information to your individual needs. The resources listed in this book are for information purposes only and such listings do not constitute referrals to these service or product providers. Publisher and/or author and or copyright holder(s) cannot be held responsible for remedies to reader for any loss or damage experienced in dealing with listed resources.

Every effort has been made to make this book as complete and as accurate as possible. However, there may be mistakes both typographical and in content. Therefore, this text should be used only as a general guide and not as the ultimate source of information. Furthermore, this book contains information available and current only up to the printing date. The purpose of this book, is to educate and entertain. The author and publisher and copyright holder(s) shall have neither liability nor responsibility to any person or entity with respect to any loss or damage caused, or alleged to be caused, directly or indirectly by the information contained in this book.

This booklet is excerpted from Leslie Zann's forthcoming book, *Outrageous Achievement*.

Cover photography by Tara Johansen.

ISBN: 978-1-0953-2782-1

Table of Contents

Foreword 1

Preface 3

Introduction 5

1. Mindset Trumps Skillset 9
2. Action vs. Right Action 11
3. Know Your Why 13
4. Develop Your Attracting Attitude 19
5. Rehire Yourself Every Week 25
6. Tackle Your Time 27
7. The Ultimate Journey 33
8. Personal Development 37

About Leslie Zann 41

Foreword

Why is it so many people have big dreams – but so few take the necessary action to make them real?

My friend, Leslie Zann, is a gifted mentor who offers sage advice, based on her extensive experience, to help you break through to success and become unstoppable.

Learning to overcome fear or limiting beliefs and how to take action is the difference between having a dream and living it.

There are people who see a way to make a big shift in their lives. And then, before they can make a move, fear or doubt sets in, and they do not take action. They abandon their dreams right at that moment of probability.

Others show great promise and get off to a fast start. They're on their way to achievement. Success is within their grasp and then, inexplicably, they do not play full out. They become stuck and don't know how to break through.

You are holding in your hands an action guide – not only to take that first step, but to stay in the game. You'll discover how to maintain confidence and resiliency in the face of all obstacles that come your way. You'll ultimately arrive at a new way of thinking. Because the thinking that got you where you are is not going to take you higher.

A winning mindset will come from an experienced mentor who has developed proven strategies. Leslie Zann is the "Outrageous Achievement" mentor who has coached and led thousands to the reality of living their dreams.

No one can take you to a place they haven't been. If they haven't sunk to the depths and clawed their way out, it is difficult to mentor anyone to do the same. If they haven't walked the road to success, they cannot lead others down it.

The road Leslie's traveled is a template for success. Let her be your guide and your mindset will shift to a place where you can create results you've never before achieved.

David Meltzer
CEO and Co-Founder, Sports 1 Marketing
Top 10 Business Coach

PREFACE

My passion is helping people discover and ignite their true and limitless potential. With more than three decades of sales, leadership and business development experience, I've gained a unique talent for helping people overcome the "limiting beliefs" that block their potential for success.

From 1986 to 1995, my then-husband and I owned a successful real estate development business, building and selling homes. After surviving two California water moratoriums on construction, everything came crashing to an end when our house burned to the ground. I literally had to pick myself up and rise from the ashes of bankruptcy, shortly thereafter a divorce, and total financial loss.

I transitioned into the direct selling profession, building a successful million-dollar organization across North America, followed by an eight-year corporate career as a national sales director and trainer. One of my colleagues said that I channel the energy of Tom Sawyer with my ability to get everyone to see that "painting the fence is fun and rewarding." This is because enthusiasm, creativity, and a can-do attitude fuel everything in my life. When I allow my heart to steer my actions, I'm able to create unprecedented success and truly unlimited possibilities. And now I teach others to do the same!

In 2012, I struck out on my own and founded Leslie Zann Consulting. I've had the privilege of speaking to over 100,000 sales entrepreneurs around the world, and reaching thousands more through the dozens of online courses I've created. My intention is to inspire you to confidently move through your fears, hesitation, or reservations, expand your vision for what's possible, and take action to create the life you desire.

This small, yet powerful booklet is a part of my mission to reach as many people as possible with the message that *everyone* has the ability to create Outrageous Achievement, reach their goals, and make their dreams come true. When you align your vision for success with my proven strategies and take action, anything is possible. You can *Grow Rich Thinking*. And when I say "Rich," I mean *Rich* in all areas of your life; health, career, relationships and creative expression. I've made it happen for myself, and I can help you make it happen too.

INTRODUCTION

What if any goal you set, or anything you wanted to be, was yours – and nothing could stand in your way?

And what if, to make this happen, you just had to be willing to spend a few hours reading a book? And of course, following the advice?

Have I piqued your interest? Good! Keep reading and let's get you to wherever you want to go; or achieving whatever goal you desire or dream that you long for.

Why don't people accomplish their goals? Or go after their dreams? What holds them back? Why are they stuck and unable to take the necessary action? Nine out of ten times, whether they realize it or not, the answer is *fear*.

Fear comes in many sizes, and can take different forms. Or a combination of modalities.

It could be fear of the unknown. Example: "There's two ways I could go and I might make the wrong choice. I'll just wait until I'm 100 percent sure."

Fear of what you do know. Example: "Based on past experience I do not have a strong belief in my ability to succeed. Think I'll sit this one out."

Fear of failure. Example: "If I don't try, I can't screw up and look like a fool. I'll let someone else take that risk."

Fear of success. Example: "If I become wealthy (and/or famous) my friends might abandon me. They seem threatened by my success. Why upset the apple cart?"

And let's not overlook: Fear of fear itself. Example: "If I always play it safe, I may not get what I want, I'll continually be settling for less, but at least I'll never have anything to be afraid of."

Notice how every fear is accompanied by an excuse – a reason to stay right where you are. A justification to *not* take action. A rationalization to stay stuck. It's a self-imposed vicious cycle.

For so many, this is the crucial choice: The choice to settle for less; or the choice to take action and get unstuck. And why so often do we *choose* to stay stuck? And yes, it is a *choice* to stay the same. It's not always a deliberate or conscious choice yet, but a choice regardless.

Simple answer: We choose to stay stuck because it's easier than facing our fears. *BAM!*

We choose to stay unhappy and dissatisfied and on the path of least resistance because it's easier than taking a risk.

Case in point: Do you have a vision for your life? Do you have dreams, goals and aspirations and yet, find yourself frequently falling short when it comes to turning those dreams into reality? What keeps derailing you? What is the unknown, intangible, unidentifiable obstacle holding you back ... keeping you from moving forward?

Your fears! And your unwillingness to harness the courage to overcome them and make a move. (Can you hear the sound track from *Jaws* playing in the background?)

So consider now – in any area of either your business or personal life – are you settling for less than you want? Less than you desire? Less that you can be? If so, it has to be negatively affecting your confidence, your psyche, your belief in yourself, and your ability to take action.

Here's the crazy part: We make up our fears. What??? They may seem real, but we really do make them up.

Here's the good news: I've learned from years of study and practice that if you can make them up, you can just as easily make them vanish. And I will show you how.

This booklet contains simple, proven strategies you can learn to dissolve your fears and create the breakthroughs you desire.

If you choose to follow the simple steps I've laid out for you here, you'll learn how to instantly harness your courage, move through your fears, begin something new or see something through, perform courageous acts; and create new, exciting opportunities for yourself.

These simple steps have worked for thousands who have taken my live seminars and courses. And now, in this booklet, they can work just as easily for you.

Are you ready to Grow Rich Thinking and experience the thrill and empowerment of living the life of your dreams? Then let's not waste another minute!

Your adventure of a lifetime begins NOW!

1
MINDSET TRUMPS SKILLSET

Whether you are gainfully employed or an entrepreneur – hold a management position or are a stay-at-home parent – a student, retired, or in career transition – this information can transform your life.

The following approaches will have a business tonality to them, and yet, you can apply the information to other aspects of your life.

Over the past 30 years, my career has been shaped through my personal experiences in sales, leading sales teams, and being an entrepreneur running my own business. I've developed a variety of skills through real estate, new home construction, direct sales, consulting, and my speaking businesses. I attribute my success largely to the two principle subjects of this chapter: Mindset and taking Action. Throughout my coaching, interestingly, I've discovered that most people who are not satisfied with their business development, advancement, achievement, or income, have convinced themselves it's their skill set that's keeping them stuck. They believe their skills are subpar and begin looking for new ways to act, speak, and relate with their new prospects, and established clients. Now don't get me wrong, staying current on trends and mastering the skills linked to your profession are necessary for long-term success. And yet, I find that in most cases, it's not a lack of skill that keeps you from realizing your true potential – but a lack of the right Mindset.

Here's the quandary: You have a clear vision on where you want to go in business and a solid commitment to reach your goals; and yet, fears and limiting beliefs are keeping you stuck!

Does it seem that for every two steps forward, you take one step back? Why are you stalled out in a roundabout of potential financial and professional success? Well, your thoughts are playing a bigger role than you may imagine.

When it comes to creating Outrageous Achievement in business – or realizing your true potential in *any* area of your life – Mindset trumps skill set every time!

2
ACTION VS. RIGHT ACTION

Throughout this booklet, you'll gain fresh clarity – and courage – to take action toward achieving your goals. Author Joel A. Barker states, "Vision without action is merely a dream."

So why are so many people in action and yet still not achieving their dreams? Because not all action is equal.

Most people know what constitutes the generic term Action: "The accomplishment of something over a period of time." Few people know what constitutes the specific term "Right Action."

"Right Action" must meet four criteria:
- Is specific and purposeful
- Moves you closer and faster to your goal
- Reflects your character, discipline, and commitment
- Creates measurable results

EXERCISE A: TAKING RIGHT ACTION

Identify a current goal you have for either your career, health, relationships or creative expression.

Goal: _____

_____

_____

What are the top three action steps you must take to turn your goal into reality?

1. _____

2. _____

3. _____

Use a separate piece of paper and complete this exercise for each action step above. Define how each step:

- Is specific and purposeful?
- Moves you closer and faster to your goal?
- Reflects your character, discipline and commitment?
- Creates measurable results?

It's easy to stay busy, preoccupied, and frenetic with your actions. This is very common for those who are not reaching the level of high achievement they desire.

When you turn ordinary action into "Right Action" your vision will move *from dream to reality* – and you will create outrageous achievement.

3
KNOW YOUR WHY

When it comes to reaching your goals or making a shift in any area of your life, do you wake up some mornings wondering, "What the hell am I doing?" Do you find yourself questioning almost every decision you make, and each action you take? Are you frustrated that you're not moving forward? Or at least not at the clip you know you're capable of? Do you wonder, "Is change even possible?"

When was the last time you tried something new? Got out of your comfort zone? Or took a bold risk? Have you lost your passion and enthusiasm; and replaced them with complacency and boredom? If so, how did that happen ... why did that happen ... and what is the solution?

I'm going to give you the Secret Sauce: One of the best ways to expedite overcoming your fears and limiting beliefs is to have a compelling WHY. With this WHY you'll get unstuck more quickly and efficiently, then make a positive shift in any area of your life, be it your career, health, relationships, or creative expression.

Let's take your career as an example. Consider this question: If time and money were no obstacle, how would your life look?

Let me help you out: Would you have the same job or career? Would your kids go to the same schools? Would you live in the same neighborhood? What would your vacations look like? What car would you be driving? And how about debt – would that disappear?

In other words, what will advancement, higher income, and more success do for your life, your family's life, and your lifestyle?

When you envision all those important areas of your life, clarity arises almost automatically – the kind of clarity that inspires you to shift your perspective and make the right moves.

When you DO NOT have a clear and compelling WHY, it's easy to be in denial. It's easy to settle for the status quo. It's easy to avoid those situations that stretch you, or make you uncomfortable. It's easy to make excuses. It's easy to procrastinate. And it's easy to not to take decisive action – it's easy to quit.

When you DO have a clear and compelling WHY, it becomes a driver of behavior, a motivator when you're feeling down or disappointed. Your clear and compelling WHY will stimulate your belief, consistency, vision, confidence, and courage. Your WHY will motivate you to take the necessary actions to create success.

Most people either ignore this concept or fatally *underestimate* the importance of keeping a clear and compelling WHY at the forefront of their mind.

To follow is a simple exercise you can do right now to clarify your WHY in your career, health, relationships, or creative expression.

EXERCISE B: CREATE YOUR WHY

What personal goals are important enough to drive my need to succeed?

_____

_____

_____

What fears or limiting beliefs have kept me from moving forward?

_____

_____

_____

What are the consequences if I don't change?

_____

_____

_____

What are the rewards if I do change?

_____

_____

_____

What vision do I hold for my career, health, relationships, or creative expression?

_____

_____

_____

How would overcoming my fear support my vision?

_____

_____

_____

What is my greatest weakness that could derail me?

_____

_____

_____

How will I overcome this?

_____

_____

_____

What greatest strength will contribute to my success?

_____

_____

_____

How will this strength support me?

_____

_____

_____

Whose help and support do I need?

_____

_____

_____

Why is this goal so important to me?

_____

_____

_____

In one sentence, what is my compelling WHY for creating success?

_____

_____

_____

When you clearly define your WHY, you'll understand what's at the heart of motivating yourself, what you want to attract into your life, and what your biggest dreams are. This clarity will give you the discipline to joyfully, authentically, consistently, and enthusiastically stay in the game and create success.

And by reviewing your WHY on a regular basis, you'll find the courage to dream bigger, set higher goals, and stay in the flow of creating bigger and better results. Your WHY drives your discipline, your accountability, your belief and your courage. It grounds you through the ups and downs of your journey and keeps you always moving forward.

Unlimited potential becomes readily possible when you are inspired by the overwhelming clarity of your own personal WHY.

4
DEVELOP YOUR ATTRACTING ATTITUDE

Once you've identified what you want "to do", the question becomes: Who will you need "to be" to carry out your plan to access your Outrageous Achievement?

When I've worked with clients who are dedicated to building a large and successful sales portfolio, I hear one consistent comment around achievement: "I'm worried I don't have what it takes to achieve my goal(s)!"

Regardless of where they are on their journey, when it comes to their ambition to be a top achiever, many just can't seem to bring that vision into clear focus.

The dialogue usually begins with: "I want to be a high achiever! I really do! I've proven myself in other areas in my life ... as a role model for my family," or "as a deacon in my church," or "as a leader in my community." And yet they admit they don't have the same confidence when it comes to becoming a top achiever in their business.

The experiential piece of achievement that's usually missing is found in the other areas of your life. You most likely walked into an established group of people where credibility and relationships had already been established. But with your sales or entrepreneurial endeavor, you get to enjoy the unique benefits of working with the ideal prospects or clients you *attract*.

So how do you become an attracting magnet? By developing an attracting attitude. Many people have no awareness of the power of an attracting attitude. They believe that their ability to create success will come from their commitment to developing more business skills.

This is a common blind spot for sales professionals who are not satisfied with the pace of their business growth. As this dissatisfaction expands, they often begin to doubt their skills. And yet, the challenge is not in your skills – but in your willingness to do what it takes to continue to attract new business prospects, or clients. In other words, your attracting attitude!

What if you were able to see things differently? What if, in reality, rather than skill, you discovered that the most important aspect of achievement is attitude?

Skill can be developed over time. But your attitude can be adjusted in a single moment of clarity!

Throughout history, when we look to the men and women who are considered "great achievers," we discover they share many common characteristics. When viewed through the lens of achievement, it becomes clear that rather than skill, attitude is the blueprint to success.

Every morning as part of my Personal Development practice, I say the following affirmation aloud. It's a daily habit that helps me set my intention to reinforce my attracting attitude:

> *"Today, the perfect people, situations and opportunities present themselves – and I am aware and open to accept them."*

EXERCISE C: DEVELOP YOUR ATTRACTING ATTITUDE

Step 1:

TODAY'S DATE: _____

I challenge you to say the affirmation at the bottom of page 20 aloud every day for 30 days. You can say it once in the morning – or you can say three times a day (morning, midday and before sleep).

Step 2:

DATE 30 DAYS LATER: _____

Describe the results you have accomplished in the past 30 days with your new attracting attitude.

_____

_____

_____

WHAT'S IN IT FOR *THEM*?

When you approach a business deal with the attitude, "What can I get?" or "What's in it for *me*?" it's simply a matter of time before the relationship disintegrates. Sooner or later, they realize your self-serving nature and how you are bringing greediness to the deal.

If, on the other hand, you show up with the attitude of "What can I give?" or "What's in it for *them*?" you set a precedent to bring authentic value to the deal. With a focus on service, you increase the odds for long-term relationships, new business, and referrals.

We all want to become the kind of professional we'd want to work with. So consider if you would work with someone whose demeanor conveys expectations such as:

- "We've got to make this happen today." (Desperate)
- "If you don't buy today – this deal is going away." (Self-serving)
- "There's nothing like it on the market." (Unrealistic promises)
- "You need to commit to a one-year order now." (High-pressure)
- "Don't worry, this is our standard contract." (Misleading)

Would you work with a professional who appears predatory? Probably not. Yet many of us have secretly struggled with how best to meet our quotas and remain authentic at the same time.

Consider your thoughts about your business prospects, or clients. In many cases, your thoughts will reveal *attachment* to certain assumptions that you have about yourself as a professional and what you expect from them.

You don't necessarily need to say your expectations out loud. Your demeanor will more times than not convey them. And that's where the real danger to your professional development lies.

When you start feeling emotions like disappointment, frustration, and regret, trace them back. Are you focused on *your* goals or those of your business prospects/clients? Are you feeling responsible for their actions? Are you emotionally attached to the outcome? Do you believe your ultimate success is based on *their* ultimate decisions?

As a professional, it's not about what you expect from your business prospects/clients – it's about what you expect from yourself!

When you can genuinely focus on their needs, you learn to detach yourself from the outcome. You learn to let go of the attachment to whatever unrealistic expectations you hold about them and their ultimate actions or decisions.

Don't get attached to attachment. Focus on modeling your personal character authentically, and in this way, all your interactions will reflect your commitment to a higher level of service, collaboration, and cooperation.

5
REHIRE YOURSELF EVERY WEEK

One of the reasons people do not reach the level of success they desire is a lack of self-accountability. If you're accustomed to someone else holding you accountable for your performance – your boss or a co-worker, your spouse or best friend – you may feel a bit lost without that support. Lost enough perhaps to avoid taking action.

So where do you find the accountability you need to achieve? What will drive you to act whether or not dire consequences are hanging over your head? *It must come from within.* You must provide it to yourself with desire, discipline and continuous activity. And yes, this is easier said than done. But like everything, it becomes easier *to do* with steady practice.

One proven method is to *rehire yourself* every week. This technique works for everyone from a full-time employee to a stay-at-home parent to an entrepreneur.

EXERCISE D: REHIRE YOURSELF EVERY WEEK

Pretend there are two of you and that one is the *boss* and the other is the *employee*.

With your *boss* hat on, evaluate the activity and productivity of your *employee* self over the past week, two weeks, or month. Be compassionate, yet honest, as you evaluate your actions, decisions, and results.

With your *boss* hat still on, decide whether or not your *employee* self deserves a raise, a warning letter, or even a pink slip. In other words, if you were your *boss*, would you give yourself a promotion? A stern lecture? Or would you fire yourself?

If you are willing to be honest with yourself, this exercise can be effective in creating clarity on whether or not you are truly in action – or if you're suffering from a lethal case of denial.

You may wonder if your *boss* self is experienced enough, knows enough to evaluate your *employee* self accurately and fairly. Your *boss* self only needs to evaluate one thing: Whether or not you are taking consistent productive action in the direction of your goals.

Years ago, I interviewed a top achiever who had set a sales record for her company. When I asked her what caused the rapid increase in her pace and productivity, she replied, "Leslie, I was convinced I was taking consistent action – until I actually started taking consistent action."

There's no silver bullet to reaching your personal and professional goals. But if there were, that would be it!

Track your consistency and your activity. Working in spurts and stops will only slow you down or worse, derail you. Consistent activity is the one gauge that will give your *boss* self the results for a fair and effective evaluation.

Have the courage to *rehire yourself* every week by putting your *boss* hat on and evaluating your actions. If your *boss* self is happy with your efforts, soon you'll tap into your unrealized potential, you'll meet and exceed your goals, and your income will skyrocket.

6
TACKLE YOUR TIME

On a scale of 1-5, with 5 being the highest, how would you rate your ability to effectively manage your time? Interestingly, this is an area where people can make a major transformation in their business (and their life) and yet, they have convinced themselves they have no options. Lack of time discipline is perpetuated when we declare, "I just don't have enough time!"

You sabotage your productivity when you dismiss your goals with an imagined time restriction.

"I would love to work with more clients" – "earn a bonus" – "increase my income" – "develop new business," *but I just don't have the time.*

Let's review three proven tips to help you shift your perspective, increase your productively, and tackle time on your terms.

AVOID AVOIDANCE

If I had a nickel for every time a professional who had not yet met their goal told me, "I am so bad at time management," I'd be richer than Oprah Winfrey (kidding, of course!). I offer you a new way to look at this excuse:

It's not that you're bad at time management – it's that you excel at avoiding the things you don't want to do! Or: It's not that you're bad at time management – rather you have a Master's Degree in Avoidance.

How do I avoid thee? Let me count the ways:

- The potential client you don't call.
- The referral you don't ask for.
- The meeting you don't schedule.
- The email you don't send.

"I am so bad at time management" is a euphemism for "I just can't find the courage to do the things that aren't simple, convenient, and fun." Or: "I just can't bring myself to do the things that make me uncomfortable, that require me to stretch, or that take me out of my comfort zone."

How do you feel when you read that last paragraph? Does it strike a chord? Have you habitually hidden behind the excuse that you are bad at time management? And in doing so have you created a self-fulfilling prophecy of avoidance, procrastination, and lack of clarity on how to move forward effectively? Change begins with awareness.

List the ways you continue to sabotage your time management.

_____

_____

_____

STOP PROCRASTINATING

You have a deadline looming. You can feel the stress building and yet, you just can't muster the discipline to act.

Your solution? You take action but it's not "Right Action." You move into a frenetic state of denial. You busy yourself with a lot of activity, but they are not the activities that will help you achieve your goals.

Procrastination is a dream stealer! It makes you squander away your valuable time and put off important tasks you should be doing, until it's too late. And then, when you realize it's too late, you panic and wish you had started earlier.

Chronic procrastinators spend years stuck in this cycle of stalling, delaying, stressing and regretting. Fear is the underlying culprit. You do everything possible to avoid what scares you, dodge rejection, and delay failure. This behavior turns into a habit and ultimately becomes pervasive in all areas of your life.

Procrastination is a damaging form of self-sabotage that chips away at your confidence, squashes your dreams, and prevents you from realizing your full potential.

You can stop allowing procrastination to be pervasive in your life with these proven strategies:

1. Divide your project into smaller steps. When something seems too overwhelming, breaking it down into several manageable steps will make it easier to take action.
2. Change your environment. Different spaces will impact your productivity. Work where you are inspired. This may even include occasionally taking your laptop with you and sitting outdoors in nature to do your work.
3. Create a detailed timeline with specific deadlines. What is the ultimate goal? What are the steps to implement for each individual action that will help you meet your timeline?
4. Work with an accountability partner. By my definition, Accountability Partners are two professionals who choose to work together, with the

ultimate goal of holding one another to a higher standard as they purposefully move their career/business forward. A relationship with an Accountability Partner can reignite and sustain your passion, because it is based on high-minded ideals. The fact that you're working peer-to-peer without a fiduciary relationship opens the door to more freedom for authenticity, idealism and openness.

5. Proudly declare your goals. It's one thing to think about them. It's another to write them down. Additionally, enthusiastically declaring your goals out loud to your boss, a co-worker, or even your spouse takes your commitment to a whole new level.

By following some or all of these tips, procrastination will become a thing of the past as you claim the vision you hold for your life and move through your fears in the direction of your dreams.

PAUSE AND PRIORITIZE

What happens when you feel the panic of not having enough hours in the day? We all know this feeling.

When this happens to me, I summon up Scotty from Star Trek, insisting to Kirk, *"I need more time, Captain!"*

You have this seemingly never-ending To Do list and yet, you can't imagine getting it all done. And your frustration keeps building because you don't know where to start. So, what do you do? Nothing! This isn't procrastination, it's paralyzation.

This is the time to stop – *breathe* – then prioritize.

Start with identifying the top priority, "MUST GET DONE" items on your list that need to be addressed first.

Then identify the lower priority items that need to get done eventually – but not before the top priority ones have been completed. Work your list accordingly.

Multitasking, or doing several things at once, is a trick we play on ourselves, thinking we're getting more done. With very few exceptions, our productivity actually decreases. As many people have discovered the hard way, multitasking isn't just inefficient, it's also stressful. So avoid this trap. Complete a project by itself; then move on to the next.

We are all busy. It's easy to get overwhelmed with your To Do list. When you find yourself unexpectedly swamped, rather than hit the panic button, remember: *breathe* – then prioritize your activities. You'll find it refreshing, even liberating, to focus on one activity at a time and see it through.

The next time you feel overwhelmed – prioritize, rather than panic – and you'll experience a lot more joy in your productivity.

7
THE ULTIMATE JOURNEY

If you could design your life – any area of your life – to be exactly as you want it, what would it look like?

In this chapter, I'm going to reveal a simple formula for creating a compelling Vision for your life. I was originally introduced to this concept by my first business coach, Jane Deuber.

What an exciting proposition to consider: If you could design any area of your life, where will you be? Who would you be with? What work would you be doing? How will you be impacting the world and making a living at the same time? What will your day look like? How much will you be earning?

The answers to these questions are the first steps to create a compelling Vision for your life and your business.

Let's consider the power inspired by VISION:

A VISION...

- Engages your heart, mind and spirit as you conceive it and bring it to fruition.
- It gives your everyday life significance and meaning.
- It's fun, invigorating and breathes new life into your journey.
- A Vision allows you to release unexpressed desires.

- It creates the discipline to take action.
- And finally, a Vision keeps you connected to your deepest desires.

One thing I know for sure is that whenever I want to improve any area of my life, there's no better way to do this than by creating a bigger Vision. You too can design your life any way you want – and here's the best part: the process is a lot of fun.

A compelling Vision is a written description of the exciting – even amazing – life you want to be living at a defined time in the future. It's a snapshot of something you want so badly that you're willing to take risks and stay in motion to see it become your reality.

Your Vision is an expression of what you will manifest in both your personal and professional life in order to make the contribution you are here to make, and live the quality of life you are here to live.

It's best if it's significant, expansive, and filled with the things that thrill and inspire you. Your Vision is your path to follow as it leads you to your greatness.

It takes commitment to gain clarity on your Vision; to see it, develop it, and articulate it. Do not put this off for another day! Begin right now to access your compelling vision with one or more of these easy tips:

Write it out on paper, in your journal or in a sketchbook. Do not be stingy with details. Go all out! The more descriptive you are the better.

Feel it by noticing the feel-good emotions your Vision evokes when you consider having all this in your life.

Picture it in a dream scrapbook, or a vision board, where you put clippings of pictures, words, and images that represent your vision. Visually capture the exciting things you want in your life.

Gather it by taking notice of significant things in your surrounding environment that you resonate with, and would love to have in your future.

Draw it using coloring pencils, paint, or crayons to express the vibrant energy you want it to include.

Take the time to work on your Vision. Don't limit your imagination with thoughts of what's "not quite right" or what's "probably wrong", or "not really possible". This is your Vision of the future you want to live into. This is not the time to play small. It's the time for limitless thinking and imagination.

Figure out where you want to make a major shift. Then create a Vision that's so compelling it moves you forward. When your Vision is bigger than your fears, you too can live life large and leap into your new future.

To begin, you must identify where in your life you are ready to live on the edge. Do you want to invest more time and effort into your career? Access the Law of Attraction with your own version of THINK, BELIEVE, ACT.

THINK: Evaluate the current situation.

BELIEVE: That you can and will create the change you want.

ACT: At a level and speed you never thought possible.

There are many ways or excuses we use to avoid living on the edge. By using this formula in the areas of your life where you want to make a shift, you can identify what's keeping you from moving towards the edge. For without living on the edge, my friend, you'll never be able to leap into the wondrous life you dream of.

Bringing your Vision to life is the ultimate journey! I encourage you to start your extraordinary adventure *today* ... and be sure to think BIG – BIGGER – BIGGEST!

8
PERSONAL DEVELOPMENT

Transformation du Jour

One day, the caterpillar knows it's time to make the shift. So it hangs itself upside down from a twig and spins a silky cocoon. Within its protective casing, the caterpillar radically transforms, and emerges as a butterfly.

For me, this is the perfect analogy for my ongoing Personal Development practice. One day, I knew it was time to make a shift. I was dissatisfied with certain areas of my life. So I turned my perception of what's possible upside down, demanding, "I want my life to be different and better!" I spun a cocoon of determination to redesign my life. My transformation began with a commitment to Personal Development. And through the process I radically reconstructed my life.

And here's the best part: Unlike the butterfly who gets just one transformation, I continue to use PD to renovate my life over and over again. It's a rejuvenating process – and one you can choose for yourself starting today.

With Personal Development a gradual process of change and expansion takes place as you live your life. Perhaps that's why even people who have reached the pinnacle of success still maintain a PD regimen.

Personal Development is the belief that you are worth the effort, time and energy needed to develop yourself.
- Denis Waitley, motivational speaker

In my experience, not a lot of people know this incredibly valuable secret: *To keep your mind fresh and open to new ideas, make Personal Development an important part of your day.* It's simple yet powerful and it opens the door to infinite potential while enriching the quality of your life at the same time.

Do not confuse Personal Development with business development – mastering the skills, strategies and concepts necessary to excel in commerce. Yes, these are important areas to actualize, but PD means working on YOU. *It's the transformative process of opening yourself up to new ideas and discoveries.* And it's one of the most life-changing gifts you can give yourself.

My clients know I don't just lecture on HOW to be successful in business, but give equal importance to having a PD support system in place to keep them well-rounded, plugged in, and both open and exposed to new ideas.

I encourage you to invest time each day – a minimum of 30 minutes – to feeding your mind with positive information and experiences that inspire you. This daily practice will have an uplifting effect on your life, and how you respond to any challenges that come your way.

If you aren't happy with the way things are – in any area of your life; from your career to your health; from your relationships to your creative expression; by making a commitment to daily PD, you can create a shift in all areas of your life.

Investing in yourself is the best investment you will ever make. It will not only improve your life, it will improve the lives of all those around you.
— **Robin Sharma, leadership expert**

There are several PD methods (or tools), and one of my favorites is reading. This is a simple practice you can begin today. I am not talking about books on leadership, although I read them and learn valuable skills and strategies for developing my administrative style. Nor am I talking about biographies of successful entrepreneurs. I love learning what it takes to cast a dream, overcome obstacles, go the distance, and turn a dream into reality.

I'm talking about books that help you understand YOU: Your thought processes, your intuition and inner guidance. These books help you expand your awareness and respond to life in new and more empowering ways. When circumstances cause you to freeze in fear – you will find the courage to face your demons. When situations push the play button on that tape in your head that recites long-standing stories of lack and disbelief – you will bravely record over them with new stories of abundance and conviction. When you are stuck – you will muster the courage to charge in the direction of your dreams.

A daily PD practice will offer you a fresh perspective. How? By thinking differently, you will act differently. I have a framed quote prominently displayed on my desk:

You are today where your thoughts have brought you; and you will be tomorrow where your thoughts take you.
— **James Allen, author**

You can't control what happens in your life, but you can control how you respond, and you can take charge of your thoughts. You can Grow Rich Thinking. This is just one of the many gifts of a Personal Development practice.

Every moment of one's existence,
one is growing into more or retreating into less.
- Norman Mailer, novelist, journalist

ABOUT LESLIE ZANN

Leslie Zann is a dynamic speaker who has presented live to more than 100,000 entrepreneurs and sales professionals around the world, and inspired thousands more through her online courses.

She founded Leslie Zann Consulting in 2012 and built a reputation as a "change maker." She is in high demand as a speaker, sales trainer, and business development coach.

A keynote speaker on the 2019 Think and Grow Rich: The Legacy World Tour, she inspires her audiences to be bold, harness their unrealized potential, and create Outrageous Achievement.

The National Speaker's Association awarded Leslie their highest honor of CSP (Certified Speaking Professional). Less than 17% of NSA members worldwide hold this prestigious title.

For a decade she was a KPBS Public Television on-air spokesperson.

Leslie is a member of the exclusive "Inner Fitness Team" at Rancho La Puerta in Tecate, Mexico, consistently voted "Best Spa in the World" by *Travel and Leisure* magazine. Leslie brings her unique approach, inspiring guests to live a life without limits.

From 2004 – 2012 she was National Director of Field Development for corporate leaders, Rodan+Fields,

Immunotec, Body Wise International, and Jockey International, where her contribution was instrumental in creating record sales and leadership development.

Her publications include: *Grow Rich Thinking* and *Choose to Be A Champion*. Her latest book, *Outrageous Achievement*, is coming soon. Leslie is a co-author of *Behind Her Brand* (Kimberley Pitts), *Best, Worst, First* (Margie Aliprandi) and *More Build It Big* (DSWA).

Leslie has a unique talent for helping individuals, entrepreneurs, and sales professionals overcome their "limiting beliefs" to create exponential success in all areas of their lives.

You can connect with Leslie on her website, social media, and by email at support@lesliezann.com.

LeslieZann.com

@LeslieZannConsulting

leslie.zann

lesliezann

Made in the USA
San Bernardino, CA
15 July 2019